FusionJuicer™

Introduction

Congratulations on your decision to purchase the Fusion Juicer™!
You have just taken a very important step towards achieving optimum health and wellness.
We are sure you will enjoy the multitude of benefits that come from incorporating more
fresh fruits and vegetables into your daily diet through juicing.

The juice recipes provided in this collection are approximations; please note the ingredient
quantities may vary depending on the ripeness and size of fruits and vegetables you use,
as well as the size of the glass.

The possibilities are endless with the Fusion Juicer™.
Have some fun experimenting by using more or less of the ingredients
listed in the recipes, or simply create your own flavor combinations according
to your personal taste.

Enjoy, and here's to your good health and wellness!

Table of Contents

Introductory Notes

The Benefits of Juicing

We are not suggesting you replace the recommended daily consumption of fruits and vegetables with juicing: they should be done in conjunction. Consuming whole fruits and vegetables daily helps you get the much needed fiber they have to offer. Juicing is just a quicker way to get many of the health benefits you need from fresh food, including antioxidants and nutrients that help your body stay healthy. It eliminates the digestion process for quicker absorption.

Get the Most From Your Fusion Juicer™

Some varieties of produce are more difficult to juice than others. The chart on page 8 will help take the guess work out of juicing. The amount of juice you create depends on which fruits and vegetables you select. Produce that doesn't yield a lot of juice should be mixed with those that do, such as oranges, apples, melons, and cucumbers.

Fresh Juice Looks Different...

You will be making FRESH JUICE... With no additives, food coloring or added sugar, it may look different from the commercially processed juice available in stores. Fresh juice tends to have a thin layer of foam on top. A quick stir with a spoon will incorporate it back into the juice or you may remove it if you prefer. To get the full benefits of fresh juice, it should be consumed within 15–20 minutes of being juiced.

The Power of Pulp

We like to say that with the Fusion Juicer™ nothing is wasted: that's why we have also included some easy "pulp friendly" food recipes for soups, muffins, salsa, and more. If you like pulp in your juice, take some from the pulp collector and add it back to your juice with a quick stir to mix it in. You can save pulp by placing it in a covered container and storing in the freezer. Keep fruit and vegetable pulp in separate containers. Do not freeze longer than 30 days.

Emptying the Pulp Collector

When juicing in large volume be sure to empty the pulp collector often. A pulp "back up" into the filter can cause the motor to shut off. Inserting a plastic bag inside the pulp collector before juicing large quantities makes for quick emptying during the process and easy clean up when you're done.

Baking Tips

- All baking times are approximate due to variations in ovens.

- Oven temperatures may be slightly hotter or colder than the temperature indicates, and this may affect baking times.

- The muffins contained in this book are loaded with fruit and fiber. They are heavy in character and not meant to be light and airy.

- Due to the heaviness of certain pulps and juices, muffins may rise then collapse once removed from the oven during the cooling process. This is normal.

General Guidelines for Juicing

Due to personal preferences and nutritional opinions, it is difficult to determine an individual's eating habits. Therefore, we recommend juicing produce the way you would normally consume it in its raw state, e.g.: remove peel from an orange. Before juicing any produce, it is important to wash it thoroughly to remove all contaminants, including soil and pesticides.

Skins, Stems and Seeds

Skins Juicing with the skins on is a personal preference with most produce.

Stems The only stems that are beneficial to process are grape stems. All others should be removed as they have no nutritional value.

Seeds Removing seeds is discretionary due to certain health risks associated with certain seeds.

Carrots

Carrots can be a bit challenging to juice due to their dense nature. Never over-stuff the chute; always leave some "wiggle room" to avoid jamming the chute. Once carrots have been inserted, replace the pusher into the chute. Apply gentle pressure to help stabilize the carrots down the chute.

Citrus Fruits

Orange and grapefruit peel is bitter in taste and should be removed. When peeling, however, leave the pith on (the white, soft layer between the peel and fruit) and juice it to get all the vitamins. Lemon and lime are used to flavor dishes, so peel may be left on for more flavor when juicing. To juice with the skin, use a slow gentle, pressure. Apply a bit more pressure if necessary, but do not use excessive force with the pusher.

Juicing Leafy Produce

Leafy produce processes best when rolled in a bunch, fed into the chute, and then followed by fruits or vegetables containing a larger volume of juice, such as celery, tomato, or cucumber. See chart page 8.

Mangos, Apricots, Peaches, Etc.

Important: Always remove pits. Do not put any produce in the juicer with pits. Pits may damage the blade, causing the motor to seize and voiding your warranty.

Pomegranates and Cherries

These wonder fruits can absolutely be juiced. When juicing cherries it is necessary to remove the pits. We recommend using a cherry pitter. When juicing pomegranate (seeds) it is necessary to separate the seeds from the outer skin and the inner membrane before they can be processed.

Pineapples and Melons

Although the juicer can process the whole fruit, it is best to cut into manageable slices. This juice tastes best when the rind is removed. Again, this is a personal preference. The "stringy" consistency of very ripe pineapple may sometimes cause blockage in the spout, requiring periodic cleaning to avoid back up and overflow in the receptacle. When juicing a pineapple we recommend removing the top and bottom of the fruit. The juicer can process most produce whole but when using larger fruits such as pineapple and melon it is best to cut them into manageable slices.

Berries and Small Fruits

Juicing berries may seem a bit challenging at first, but once you get the hang of it you will love the great flavors they add to your juice — not to mention the health benefits they have to offer. When juicing berries (except cranberries) you will need to add something that contains a larger volume of juice such as an apple or orange. For example, process the berries first (you may not see a lot of juice come out at first) then add something that is juicy — like an apple or an orange — and you will see the berry juice come pouring out.

Smoothies

• When making smoothies, juice first with the Fusion Juicer™. Then add the fresh juice, ice and desired ingredients in a blender. This juicer will not make smoothies — only fresh juice for smoothies.

• Bananas are used in most of our smoothie recipes. Add bananas separately into a blender to blend with other juices. Do not put bananas in the Fusion Juicer™ as they will not make juice. The Fusion Juicer™ will not make smoothies — only fresh juice for smoothies.

Important Information About Sweetener or Sweeteners

We do not recommend artificial sweeteners.

The recipes in this book use agave as the main sweetener. We use agave, but you can use other sweeteners of your choice. We have included a sweetener conversion chart below that includes stevia, agave, sugar, and honey. We chose these four sweeteners as our top picks. There is continuous research done on new sweeteners as well as the ones that we have listed. Therefore, we leave it up to the consumer to decide what sweetener is best for you. For a healthier alternative, use apples to sweeten any fruit or vegetable juice.

Sweeteners Chart

Note: This chart is an estimated conversion chart based on 1 c. sugar.

1 c. Sugar = 1 tsp. Stevia Powder or Liquid

1 c. Sugar = 2/3 c. Agave

1 c. Sugar = 1/2 c. Honey

Produce Chart

Apple	Grapefruit	Peach (firm)
Asparagus	Guava	Pear (firm)
Brussels sprout	Honeydew melon	Pepper
Cabbage	Horseradish	Pineapple (firm)
Cantaloupe	Jicama	Pomegranate seed
Celery	Kiwi (firm)	Potato
Cherry (pitted)	Kohlrabi	Pumpkin
Clementine	Lemon	Radicchio
Cranberry	Lettuce	Radish
Cucumber	Lime	Squash
Fennel	Nectarine (firm)	Strawberry
Garlic	Onion	Tangerine
Ginger	Orange	Tomato (firm)
Grape	Parsnip	Watermelon

Fruits and Vegetables More Challenging to Juice

Apricot	Green bean	Parsley
Basil	Green pea	Passion fruit
Beet	Kale	Peppermint
Blackberry	Leafy green	Plum
Blueberry	Leek	Raspberry
Broccoli	Mango	Spinach
Carrot	Mint	Swiss chard
Cauliflower	Mushroom	Turnip
Collard green	Mustard green	Watercress
Dandelion green	Okra (skin removed)	Wheatgrass
Endive	Papaya	

Fruits and Vegetables Containing a Large Juice Content

Apple	Grape	Pepper
Cantaloupe	Grapefruit	Pineapple
Celery	Honeydew melon	Tangerine
Clementine	Lemon	Tomato
Cranberry	Lime	Watermelon
Cucumber	Orange	

Some fruits and vegetables cannot be juiced due to their inability to produce juice. Although they are unable to be juiced, that does not mean we should not enjoy them as whole foods on a daily basis as part of a healthy diet. Examples are avocado, banana and coconut.

Never use the green tops of rhubarb. The oxalic acid in the leaves is toxic. There are so many other healthy fruits and vegetables available that it's just easier and safer to skip rhubarb as a juice source.

Never add any liquids of any kind into the juicer.

Juice & Pulp Yield Per Produce

Apples
6 medium apples = 2 c. juice
6 medium apples = 1 1/2 c. pulp

Carrots
5 large carrots = 1 c. juice
5 large carrots = 1 c. pulp

Celery Stalks
4 celery stalks = 3/4 c. juice
4 celery stalks = 1/4 c. pulp

Cucumbers
1 large cucumber = 1 c. juice
1 large cucumber = 1/3 c. pulp

Mangos
6 mangos = 2 1/2 c. juice
6 mangos = 2 c. pulp

Oranges
5 medium oranges = 2 c. juice
5 medium oranges = 1 1/2 c. pulp

Papayas
1 medium papaya = approx 1/2 c. juice
1 medium papaya = 1/3 c. pulp

Passion Fruits
4 passion fruits = 1/4 c. juice
4 passion fruits = 1/2 c. pulp

Pears
6 medium pears = 2 c. juice
6 medium pears = 1 1/2 c. pulp

Pineapples
2 medium pineapples = approx. 2 c. juice
2 medium pineapples = 2 1/2 c. pulp

Potatoes
8 medium red potatoes = 2 1/2 c. juice
8 medium red potatoes = approx. 2 c. pulp

Raspberries

1/2 pt. raspberries = approx. 1/2 c. juice
1/2 pt. raspberries = approx. 1/4 c. pulp

Strawberries
1 qt. approx. 30 strawberries = 2 c. juice
1 qt. approx. 30 strawberries = 1/3 c. pulp

Tomatoes
4 medium firm tomatoes = 2 c. juice
4 medium firm tomatoes = 1 c. pulp

Zucchinis and Squashes
5 small zucchinis/squashes = approx. 1 c. juice
5 small zucchinis/squashes = approx. 1/2 c. pulp

Simply Carrot

4 large carrots (tops removed)
1 large celery stalk

Carrot Juice

5 large carrots (tops removed)

Cucumber & Carrot Juice

2 large carrots (tops removed)
1 medium cucumber (peeled)

SIMPLY CARROT

FusionJuicer™

Apple Juice

3 large apples

Mix sweet and tart apples for best flavor.
Spice it up with a sprig of mint or a slice of ginger.

Pineapple
& Carrot Juice

4 large carrots (tops removed)
1/2 pineapple (rind & core removed)

Grape Juice

1 bunch seedless white or red grapes

Fusion Juicer™

Sweet
Juice Sensation

1 orange (peeled)
1 sweet apple
1 large carrot (top removed)
1 grapefruit (peeled)
1/2 cantaloupe (peeled & seeded) or 1 pear

Tropical Blend

1 guava (peeled & pitted)
1 papaya (peeled & seeded)
1 pineapple spear (rind removed)
1 large orange (peeled)
1 mango (peeled & pitted)

Fusion Juicer

Cucumber Mint

2 cucumbers (peeled)
1 bunch mint

Pineapple Orange Blast

4 pineapple spears (rind removed)
1 medium orange (peeled)

Carrot, Apple & Ginger

2 medium carrots (tops removed)
1 apple
1" piece ginger (peeled)

If you like spicy juice add more ginger!

Carrot Fruit Juice

4 large carrots (tops removed)
2 apples

FusionJuicer™

Country Lemonade

3 large lemons (peel intact)
5 tbsp. honey
4 c. spring water

Juice the lemons. Add honey and water to juice. Pour over crushed ice.

Sugarless Lemonade

2 medium apples
1/2 lemon (peel intact)

FusionJuicer™

Melon Combo

1/2 cantaloupe (peeled & seeded)
1/2 honeydew (rind removed & seeded)
1/2 seedless watermelon (rind removed)
1 bunch mint

Cut into manageable pieces that will fit into chute.

Papaya Surprise

1 papaya (peeled & seeded)
1 pineapple (rind & core removed)

Papaya Juice

1 large papaya (peeled & seeded)

FusionJuicer™

Orange Juice

5 large oranges (peeled)

Blood
Orange Juice

5 large blood oranges (peeled)

Pine-Go

4 pineapple spears (rind removed)
1 mango (peeled & pitted)

FusionJuicer

Vitamin C Boost

2 large oranges (peeled)
2 large grapefruits (peeled)

South of the Border

1/4 large red bell pepper
1 celery stalk
1/2 lime (peeled)
few sprigs cilantro
1 small apple

Super Juice

1/2 pineapple spear (rind removed)
1 large orange (peeled)
1 papaya or 1 mango (peeled, seeded or pitted)
2 large carrots (tops removed)
1/2 lime (peeled)

FusionJuicer™

Pear & Grape Juice

2 pears
1/2 doz. seedless white grapes
4 collard greens

Power Punch

2 c. kale
2 c. parsley
1 c. spinach leaves
1 medium apple
3 celery stalks
1/2 green bell pepper

Fusion Juicer™

Raspberry Rush

2 pt. raspberries
1 large orange (peeled)
1 medium lime (peeled)

Serve over crushed ice.

Breakfast
Pick Me Up

1/2 cantaloupe (peeled & seeded)
1 large carrot (top removed)
1/2 lime (peel intact)
1 small apple

FusionJuicer™

Carrot & Beet Juice

1 beet (leaves removed)
3 carrots (tops removed)

Beach Body

3 carrots (tops removed)
2 celery stalks
1/2 cucumber (peeled)
1/2 c. parsley
1 small beet (leaves removed)
1 small apple

Passion Play

1 passion fruit
1 c. seedless red grapes
1 kiwi (peeled)
1/2 c. strawberries (hulled)

CARROT & BEET JUICE

FusionJuicer™

Cucumber
Pear Pineapple

1 cucumber (peeled)
1 pineapple spear (rind removed)
1 Bartlett pear
2 kale leaves

Summer Punch

1 pt. strawberries (hulled)
1/2 pineapple (rind & core removed)
bunch seedless red grapes

Serve over crushed ice.

Berry Fizz

1 c. cranberries
1 c. strawberries (hulled)
1 c. raspberries

Juice ingredients then pour the mixture into a glass with 1 c. sparkling apple cider.

FusionJuicer™

Papaya & Aloe Juice

1 papaya (peeled & seeded)
3" piece aloe (rind removed)

Spicy Orange

1" piece ginger (peeled)
2 large oranges (peeled)
1/2 cantaloupe (peeled & seeded)
1/2 lemon (peel intact)

Fusion Juicer™

Energy Boost

1 carrot (top removed)
1 celery stalk
1 beet (leaves removed)
5 parsley springs
4 lettuce leaves
1/2 head watercress
1/2 c. spinach
3 tomatoes
salt to taste

Kiwi Kooler

2 kiwis (peeled)
1/2 pineapple (rind & core removed)
1 orange (peeled)
1" piece ginger (peeled)

For a special treat, juice ingredients and then separately stir in coconut milk.

ENERGY BOOST

FusionJuicer™

Achy
Breaky Juice

1/4 turnip
1/4 green bell pepper
2 apples
1/2 cup blueberries

Rainbow
Surprise

1 celery stalk
4 carrots (tops removed)
1 cucumber (peeled)
1 yellow squash
1 zucchini
1 sweet apple

Serve over ice.

Clean Sweep

1/2 lemon (peel intact)
1 apple
1/2 beet (leaves removed)
1 large celery stalk
1/4 cucumber (peeled)

Fusion Juicer™

Cool-down Splash

3 carrots (tops removed)
3 strawberries (hulled)
1 passion fruit
3 cauliflower florets
1/4 red cabbage

Stress Buster

2 celery stalks
1/2 bulb fennel
2 c. romaine lettuce
1/2 pineapple (rind & core removed)

Cantaloupe Calmer

1/2 cantaloupe (peeled & seeded)
2 pears

Juice ingredients, then add coconut milk separately for an exotic treat.

FusionJuicer™

Daily Detox

6 asparagus stalks (trimmed)
1/2 lemon (peel intact)
1/2 cucumber (peeled)

Alternatives to asparagus: endive, watercress.

Apple Celery Juice

2 apple
3 carrots (tops removed)
2 celery stalks

Papple Juice

1/2 papaya (peeled & seeded)
1 pineapple spear (rind removed)
1 nectarine (pitted)

FusionJuicer™

Digestive Jump Start

1/2 papaya (peeled & seeded)
1 apple
1 guava (peeled & pitted)

Orangeberry

1 orange (peeled)
2 kiwis (peeled)
6 strawberries (hulled)

Pineberry Juice

8 strawberries (hulled)
3 pineapple spears (rind removed)
2 kiwis (peeled)

Fusion Juicer™

Healthy Glow

1/4 cucumber (peeled)
1 c. blueberries
3 passion fruit
1 pineapple spear (rind removed)

Sweet Beet

1 apple
1/2 beet (leaves removed)
3 carrots (tops removed)

Healthy Heart

2 oranges (peeled)
3 Brussels sprouts
1 bunch seedless red grapes
1 small or 1/2 large pomegranate (seeds)

FusionJuicer

Immunoblast

3 strawberries (hulled)
1 orange (peeled)
1 apple
1 apricot (pitted)
3 broccoli florets
3 cauliflower florets

Cabbage Cleanser

2 apples
2 carrots (tops removed)
1/2 head cabbage

Cran-grape

1 bunch seedless red grapes
2 c. cranberries

IMMUNOBLAST

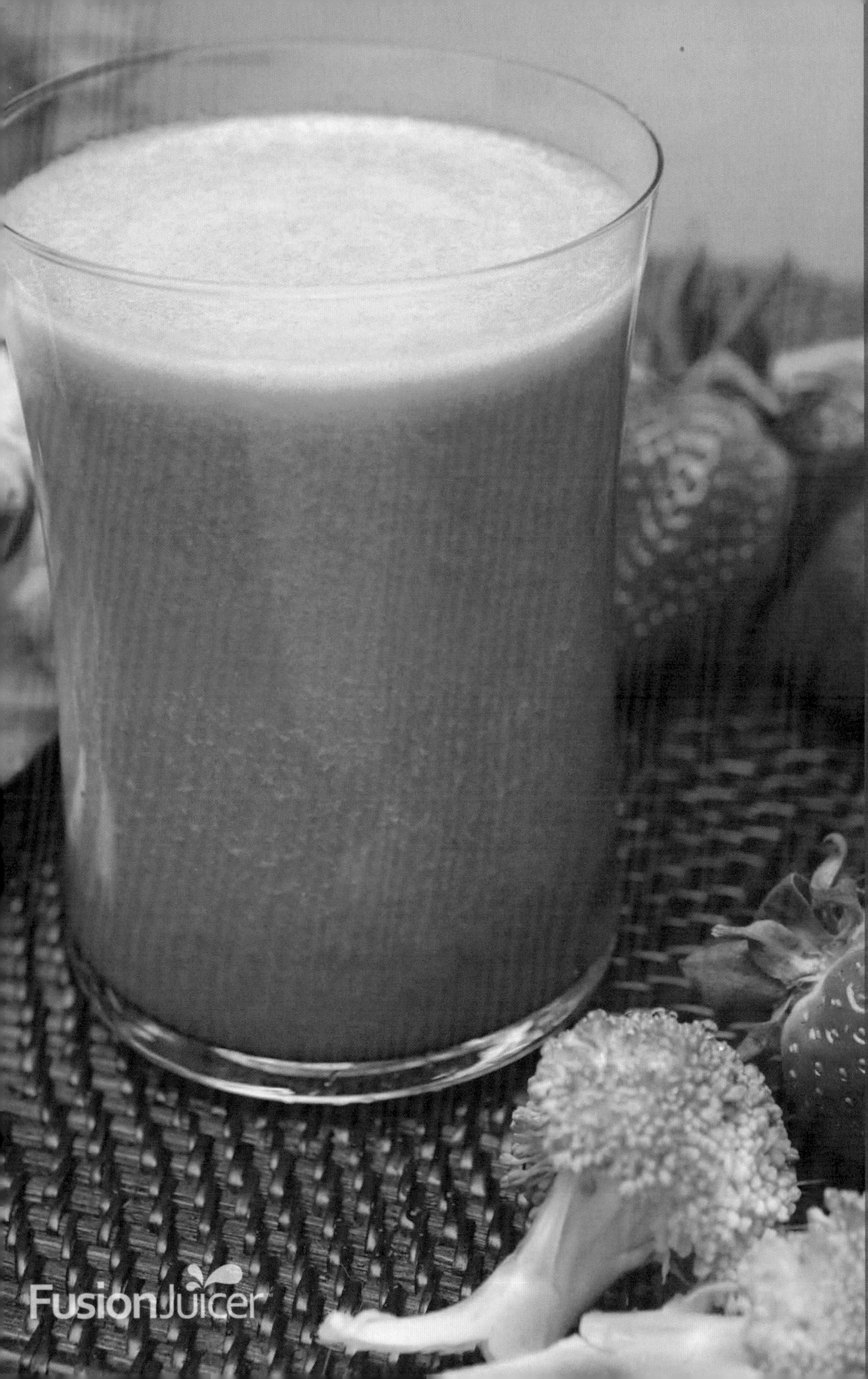

Fruity 5

1 orange (peeled)
1/2 lime (peeled)
2 pineapple spears (rind removed)
3 strawberries (hulled)
1/2 kiwi (peeled)

Pear-Fect

1 pear
1 peach (pitted)
1 c. cranberries
1/2 pineapple (rind & core removed)

Power Up

4 celery stalks
1/2 cucumber (peeled)
1/2 c. spinach leaves
1 medium apple
1/2 green bell pepper

FusionJuicery

Super 7

2 carrots (tops removed)
1 potato
2 broccoli florets
1/2 small beet (leaves removed)
1/4 red bell pepper
1 tomato
1/4 cucumber (peeled)

Tract Teaser

1 Granny Smith apple
1 Red Delicious apple
2 bunches seedless white grapes
2 bunches seedless red grapes
1/2 cup cranberries

Cucumber Cooler

1 apple
2 cucumbers (peeled)

Fusion Juicer

Lighten Up

1/2 apple
1/4 cantaloupe (peeled & seeded)
Six 3" cubes seedless watermelon (rind removed)
1/2 grapefruit (peeled)

The Big C

1 orange (peeled)
1 apple
1 c. cherries (pitted & stemmed)

Fusion Juicer™

Mama Mia

2 oranges (peeled)
1 beet (leaves removed)
2 broccoli florets
2 oranges (peeled)

Double Dose

1/2 pomegranate (seeds)
1 apple
1 c. cherries (pitted & stemmed)

Plum Surprise

1 apricot (pitted)
1 apple
3 plums (pitted)

FusionJuicer™

Mood Attack

3 pineapple spears (rind removed)
1 passion fruit
Four 3" cubes seedless watermelon (rind removed)

Celery Blend

1 celery head
1 large carrot (top removed)
1 lemon wedge (peel intact)

Good Morning Delight

1 large carrot (top removed)
1 medium Red Delicious apple
1 pt. strawberries (hulled)

FusionJuicer™

Seeing
Is Believing

1/2 papaya (peeled & seeded)
2 carrots (tops removed)
1 mango (peeled & pitted)

Peachy Keen

1 peach (pitted)
2 apricots (pitted)
1 pear
1 small apple

FusionJuicer™

Think Drink

1 passion fruit
1 apple
1" piece of ginseng

Purely Plum

1 apple
4 plums (pitted)

Bone Aid

1 c. cherries (pitted & stemmed)
1 sweet potato
1/4 turnip

Throat Coat

1 handful wheat grass wrapped in kale leaf
1 lemon (peel intact)
3 pineapple spears (rind removed)

Cherry Cooler

1 1/2 c. cherries (pitted)

Pour cherry juice into a glass with 1 c. sparkling mineral water.

Raspberry Treat

1 orange (peeled)
One 3″ cube seedless watermelon (rind removed)
2 c. raspberries

FusionJuicer™

Under
the Weather

1 orange (peeled)
1 lemon (peel intact)
1" piece of ginger (peeled)
1 guava (peeled & pitted)

Tropical Surprise

1/2 pt. raspberries
1 mango (peeled & pitted)
6 pineapple spears (rind removed)
1 papaya (peeled & seeded)
1 kiwi (peeled)

Sweet Dreams

1 cherries (pitted & stemmed)
1/2 passion fruit

Pour mixture into a cup with steeped chamomile tea.

Sweet Nectarine

1 orange (peeled)
1 nectarine (pitted)
2 c. raspberries

FusionJuicer™

Sunset

2 carrots (tops removed)
1 orange (peeled)
1 pear
1 red potato

Tomato Juice

3 lb. tomatoes

Spice it up: Add a few stalks of celery and fresh ground pepper to taste.

Fusion Juicer™

Prickly Pear Delight

1 prickly pear
1 lemon (peel intact)
1 pineapple spear (rind removed)

Breakfast Eye Opener

4 pineapple spears (rind removed)
1 pink grapefruit (peeled)

PRICKLY PEAR DELIGHT

FusionJuicer

Vegetable Juice Potluck

1 tomato
2 celery stalks
2 large carrots (tops removed)
5 large broccoli florets
1/2 cucumber (peeled)

Juicer Ginger Ale

1" piece ginger (peeled)
1/2 cantaloupe (peeled & seeded)
1/2 pt. strawberries (hulled)
1 orange (peeled)

Add 1 c. sparkling water separately. Mix well.

FusionJuicer™

Fruit Juice
Surprise

1 bunch seedless red grapes
1 apple
1 orange (peeled)
1/4 cantaloupe (peeled & seeded)

Paradise Island

1 papaya (peeled & seeded)
1 orange (peeled)
1/2 pineapple (rind & core removed)
1 lime (peel intact)
1" piece ginger (peeled)

FRUIT JUICE SURPRISE

Fusion Juicer™

Wheat Grass Energy Drink

1 handful wheat grass
1 handful spinach
1 pineapple spear (rind removed)

Super Boost

3 tomatoes
1/4 red bell pepper
1/4 green bell pepper
2 garlic cloves (peeled)
1/4 jalapeño pepper
1/4 onion (peeled)
1 celery stalk

WHEAT GRASS ENERGY DRINK

Booster Shot

2 oranges (peeled)
1 lemon (peel intact)
1″ piece ginger (peeled)

Love Potion

1 peach (pitted)
1 c. seedless red grapes
1 c. strawberries (hulled)
1 small apple

Fusion Juicer

Red Zinger

1 beet (leaves removed)
2 limes (peel intact)
1" piece ginger (peeled)

Cran-Apple

1 c. cranberries
2 medium apples

RED ZINGER

Juicy
Adrenaline Rush

1 lemon (peel intact)
1 orange (peeled)
1 pineapple spear (rind removed)
Three 3" cubes seedless watermelon (rind removed)

Watermelon Juice

1/2 seedless watermelon (rind removed)

Cut watermelon into pieces that will fit easily into chute.

Fusion Juicer

One Potato Sweet Potato

1 orange (peeled)
1 pear
2 carrots (tops removed)
1 sweet potato

Super Sunrise

3 pineapple spears (rind removed)
1/2 orange (peeled)
4 strawberries (hulled)
1 bunch seedless red grapes

Tropical Teaser

2 mangos (peeled & pitted)
1 papaya wedge (peeled & seeded)
1 pineapple spear (rind removed)
5 strawberries (hulled)
1 kiwi (peeled)

Skin Glow

1 cucumber (peeled)
1/2 c. parsley
1 small apple
4 carrots (tops removed)

*Juice ingredients, then add 1/4 – 1/2 c. coconut milk or soy milk separately.
Mix well*

FusionJuicer™

Prickly Pear Juice

1 bunch seedless red grapes
1 lemon (peel intact)
2 prickly pears

Cool & Light

2 large cucumbers (peeled)
2 large carrots (tops removed)
1 sweet apple
1/2 lemon (peeled)

FusionJuicer™

Green Machine

1 cucumber (peeled)
3 broccoli florets
1 kiwi (peeled)
1 bunch seedless white grapes

Salad in a Glass

1 tomato
1/2 head leaf lettuce
2 celery stalks
1 carrot (top removed)

FusionJuicer™

Berry Bonanza

1 c. blueberries
1 c. raspberries
2 oranges (peeled)

Mango Surprise

1 mango (peeled & pitted)
2 kiwis (peeled)
1 large carrot (top removed)

Hot Tomato

1 medium tomato
1 medium carrot (top removed)
1 celery stalk
1" piece ginger (peeled)
1" piece horseradish
few sprigs fresh cilantro
1 radish (top removed)
1 garlic clove (peeled)
Season with salt and pepper to taste.

Add vodka to juice separately for a great Bloody Mary.

BERRY BONANZA

Sweet Surprise

3 pineapple spears (rind removed)
1 orange (peeled)
4 strawberries (hulled)
1 bunch seedless red grapes

Peach
& Pear Blend

2 peaches (pitted)
1 pear

Lunch
in a Glass

2 tomatoes
2 carrots (tops removed)
1/2 head cabbage
2 celery stalks
1 broccoli head

Cherry Zest

1 lemon (peeled)
1/2 lime (peeled)
2 passion fruit
2 c. cherries (pitted & stemmed)

FusionJuicer™

South Sea Island

1 papaya (peeled & seeded)
1 kiwi (peeled)
6 strawberries (hulled)
1 pineapple spear (rind removed)

Strawberry & Pear Champagne

1 pt. strawberries (hulled)
1 pear

*Juice ingredients, then add seltzer or dry,
white champagne separately in glass. Mix well.*

Fusion Juicer™

Lemon
Lime Zip

1 lemon (peeled)
1 lime (peeled)
2 pears

Strawberry
Special

5 large strawberries (hulled)
1/2 pt. raspberries
1/2 lemon (peeled)

Add sparkling mineral water, ginger ale, or champagne to juice separately in a glass.

Fusion Juicer™

Melon Delight

One 3″ cube seedless watermelon (rind removed)
1 pineapple spear (rind removed)
2 cantaloupe wedge (peeled & seeded)
4 strawberries (hulled)

Fruit Fizz

1/2 lb. raspberries
1 medium orange (peeled)
1/4 lime (peeled)
1/2 pineapple (rind & core removed)

Juice ingredients then add seltzer, ginger ale, or champagne separately.

Apple Fizz

4 large apples

Juice apples then add 10 oz. sparkling mineral water or champagne separately.

FusionJuicer™

Afternoon Zing

1/2 broccoli head
1/4 lemon (peel intact)
1/2 bunch seedless red grapes
1 pear

Peppery Punch

2 celery stalks
4 radishes (top removed)
2 tomatoes
1/2 jalapeño pepper

AFTERNOON ZING

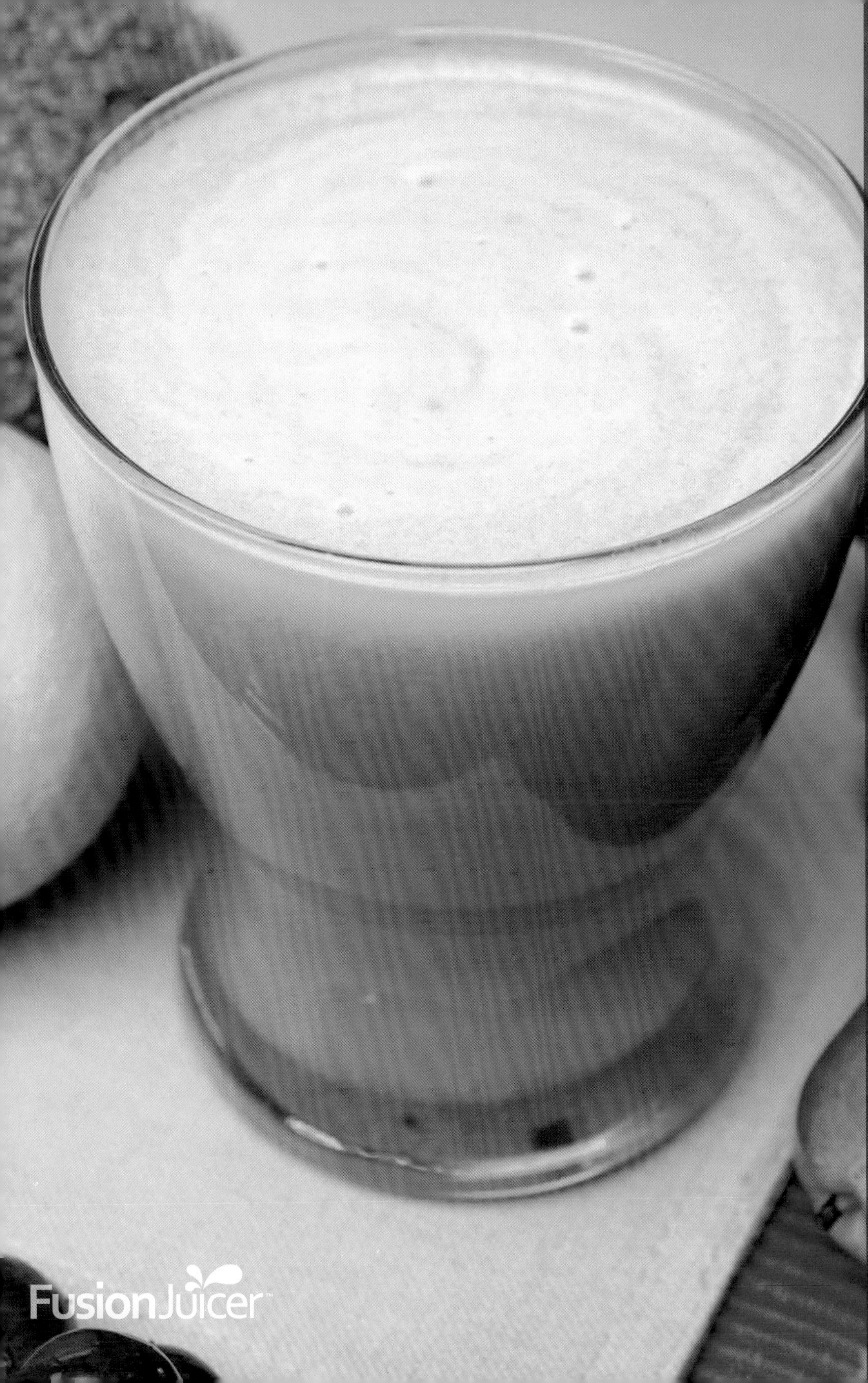

Morning Tonic

1 grapefruit (peeled)
2 carrots (tops removed)
1/2" piece ginger (peeled)
5 prunes

Sunrise Salute

2 small green apples
1 small pear
6 prunes

FusionJuicer™

Juicy Daiquiri

1 c. strawberries (hulled)
1 c. blackberries
One 3" cube seedless watermelon (rind removed)

Cleansing Remedy

1/4 small head cabbage
2 carrots (tops removed)
1" piece ginger (peeled)

Fusion Power

Berrytini

One 3" cube seedless watermelon (rind removed)
1 bunch seedless red grapes
1 orange (peeled)
1 c. raspberries
1 c. blueberries

Veggie Kick

2 tomatoes
1" piece horseradish
2 mushrooms
2 carrots (tops removed)

FusionJuicer

Craving Killer

1 celery stalk
1 medium tomato
4 asparagus (trimmed)
1 orange (peeled)
1/2 leak (white only)

California Dream

1/4 cantaloupe (peeled & seeded)
1/2 cucumber (peeled)
1 handful wheat grass

FusionJuicer

Cucumber Spa Cocktail

1 small pear
1 pineapple spear (rind removed)
1 small yellow bell pepper
1 English cucumber (peeled)
1 lemon (peel intact)

Clear Shock

1/2" piece horseradish
20 mint leaves
30 cilantro leaves
1 carrot (top removed)
1 orange (peeled)
1 apple

FusionJuicer

Iron Man

1 c. parsley
1 small green apple
4 broccoli florets
3 celery stalks
1/2 lemon (peel intact)

Tomato Caliente

3 tomatoes
1/2 green bell pepper
1/2 jalapeño pepper

Fusion Juicer™

Veggie Garden

1 small tomato
1 carrot (top removed)
1 small red bell pepper
1 sweet potato
2 celery stalks

K-Boost

1 parsnip (top removed)
1 carrot (top removed)
1 endive

juicer

Pomegranate-Blueberry Juice

1/2 c. pomegranate (seeds)
1 c. blueberries
1 small bunch grapes

Tropical Squeeze

1 tangerine (peeled)
1 passion fruit
1/2 grapefruit (peeled)

POMEGRANATE-BLUEBERRY JUICE

SensationJuicer

Fruitilicious

1 cantaloupe wedge (peeled & seeded)
6 strawberries (hulled)
1" piece ginger (peeled)

Summer Refresher

1 star fruit
1 tangerine (peeled)
1/2 mango (peeled & pitted)

FRUITILICIOUS

fusionjuicer

Razzle Dazzler

1 c. raspberries
1/2 lemon (peel intact)
1 pineapple spear (rind removed)

*Separately add sparkling mineral water to juice. Serve over ice,
garnish with sprig of mint and an additional 1/2 c. whole raspberries.*

Beetphrodisiac

2 beets (leaves removed)
1/4 bulb fennel
1/3 c. parsley

FusionJuicer

Pomegranate Punch

1 pineapple spear (rind removed)
1 pomegranate (seeds)
1 orange (peeled)

Pomegranate Berry

1/4 pomegranate (seeds)
3/4 c. blueberries
3/4 c. raspberries
1 green apple
1 red apple

Optional: Serve over sparkling water and ice.

FusionJuicer

Jumpin' Juice

1/2 yam (peeled)
2 tomatoes
1 carrot (top removed)
1 garlic clove (peeled)
1" piece ginger (peeled)

Yummy Tummy

1/2" piece aloe (rind removed)
1 large papaya (peeled & seeded)
1" piece ginger (peeled)
1 apple

JUMPIN' JUICE

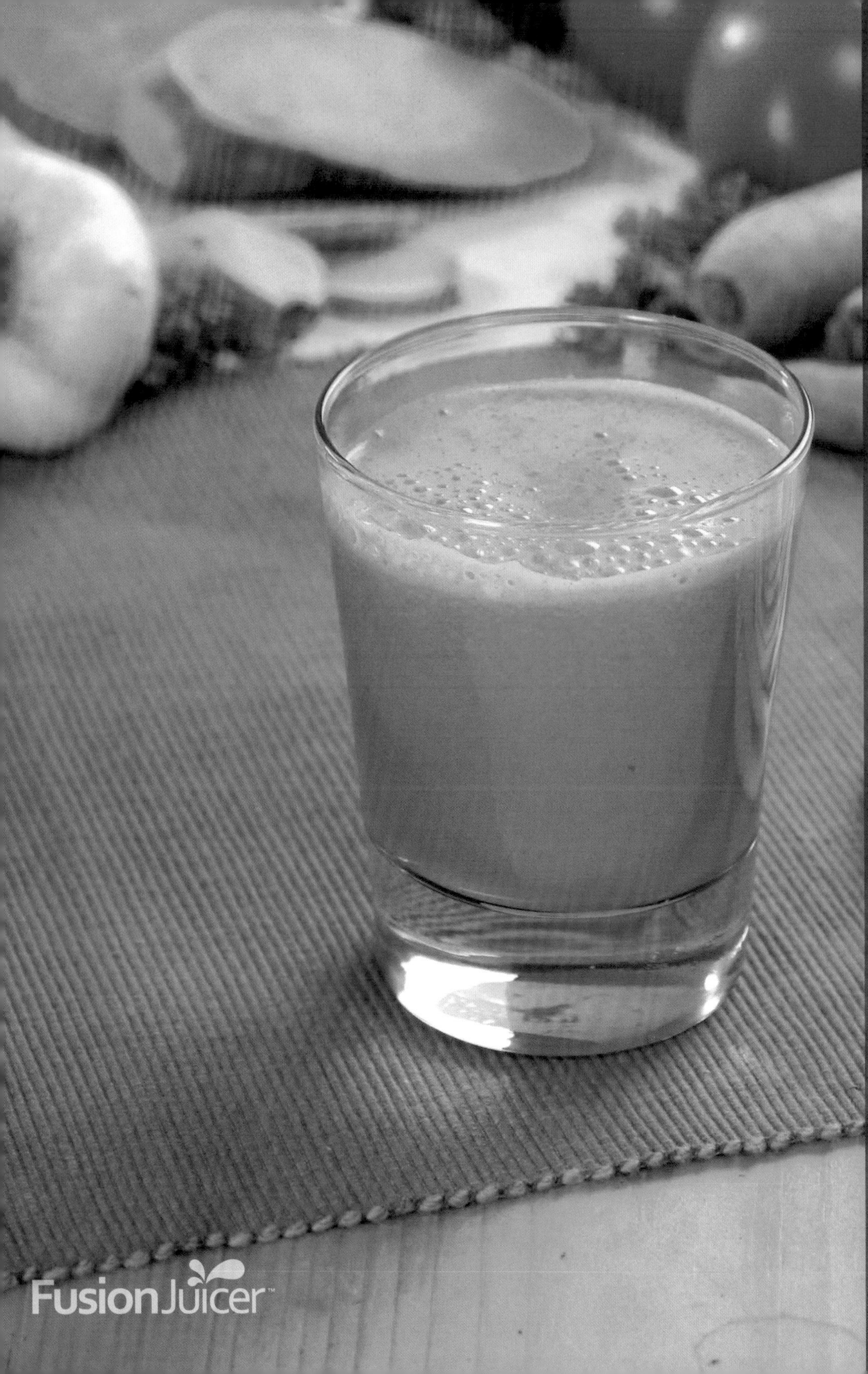

FusionJuicer™

Boost Juice

1 small red apple
1 lemon (peel intact)
1/2 mango (peeled & pitted)
10 strawberries (hulled)
1 small pear

Island Illusion

1/2 small papaya (peeled & seeded)
6 strawberries (hulled)
1/2 mango (peeled & pitted)
1 kiwi (peeled)

Optional: Serve over sparkling water and ice.

Melon Shooters

One 3" cube seedless watermelon (rind removed)
1 honeydew wedge (rind removed & seeded)
1 cantaloupe wedge (peeled & seeded)

Juice each separately and pour into shooter glasses.

Fab Heart

1 zucchini
2 large broccoli florets
1 garlic clove (peeled)
2 tomatoes

Fusion Juicer

ISLAND SMOOTHIE

FusionJuicer

Island Smoothie

6 strawberries (hulled)
2 pineapple spears (rind removed)
1 star fruit
2 large bananas (peeled)
1 c. coconut water

Juice the first 3 ingredients. In a blender, add juice, banana, and coconut water. Blend until creamy.

Papaya, Guava, Pineapple Smoothie

1/4 c. pineapple juice
1/2 c. papaya juice
1/2 c. guava juice
1 tsp. pulp from each fruit

After juicing the first three fruits separately, use a blender to mix all ingredients until creamy.

Tropical Delight

1/4 c. pineapple juice
1/2 c. papaya juice
1/2 c. mango juice
2 large bananas (peeled)
1 tsp. pulp from each fruit

In a blender, mix all ingredients until creamy.

TROPICAL SMOOTHIE

FusionJuicer

Tropical Smoothie

1/2 pt. raspberries
1 mango (peeled & pitted)
1/2 pineapple (rind & core removed)
1/2 papaya (peeled & seeded)
1 kiwi (peeled)
1 c. ice
1/2 c. coconut water
1 banana (peeled)
3 tbsp. wheat germ

*Juice the first five ingredients. In a blender mix juice
and the rest of the ingredients. Blend to thick consistency.*

Mango, Raspberry, Rush Smoothie

1/2 c. mango juice
1/3 c. raspberry juice
2 large bananas (peeled)
1 tsp. mango pulp
1 tsp. raspberry pulp
1/4 c. acai puree
1 c. ice

In a blender, mix all ingredients until creamy.

Super C

1/2 c. strawberry juice
1/2 c. orange juice
3 large bananas (peeled)
1 tsp. strawberry pulp
1 tsp. orange pulp
1 c. ice

In a blender, mix all ingredients until creamy.

Beauty Bonanza

2 cucumbers (peeled)
1 lemon (peel intact)
1 avocado (peeled & pitted)
1 c. ice

Juice lemon and cucumbers first, then add avocado
and ice separately in the blender. Blend well.

Grapefruit Smoothie

1/3 c. pineapple juice
1/4 c. grapefruit juice
3 tbsp. strawberry juice
1 banana (peeled)
1 c. ice

In a blender, mix all ingredients until creamy.

Sweet Dreams

1" piece ginger (peeled)
3 celery stalks
1/2 small head cabbage
1 green bell pepper
1 medium apple
1 banana (peeled)
1 c. ice
1/2 c. skim milk or milk substitute

Juice all ingredients except for the ice, milk, and banana. Mix in blender with banana, ice, and skim milk (or substitute milk of your choice, use soy milk for added health benefits).

FROZEN FRUIT POPS

Frozen Fruit Pops

Experiment with fresh fruit juice and pulp to make tasty frozen treats. For juicy fruit pops mix juice with pulp and freeze. There is no right or wrong way; do it however you like it. Experiment with different fruits to make healthy pops. You can have fun by mixing flavors as well.

Orange Pops
4 oranges (peeled)

Cherry Pops
4 cups cherries (pitted & stemmed)
3/4 cups pulp

Pineapple Pops
1 pineapple (rind & core removed)
1/2 cup pulp

Watermelon Pops
1/4 seedless watermelon (rind removed)
3/4 cup pulp

*Juice the fruits. Mix the juice and pulp together if the recipe requires it.
Pour into ice cube trays. Cover the tray with plastic wrap. Poke popsicle sticks through the plastic wrap into the center of each section of the ice cube trays so that it reaches about halfway into the juice mixture. The plastic wrap will help hold the stick straight up. Freeze and serve. You can also use your favorite ice pop molds.*

Frozen Fruit Cubes

Freeze fruit juice for cubes to flavor water, juice, sparkling water, seltzer or champagne. Try champagne with a frozen strawberry fruit cube.

ORANGE & WATERMELON ICE

Orange Ice

4 oranges (peeled)

Juice the fruits. Pour into dessert dish and freeze.

Watermelon Ice

1/4 seedless watermelon (rind removed)

Juice the fruits. Pour into dessert dish and freeze.

Pineapple Ice

1/2 pineapple (rind & core removed)

Juice the fruits. Pour into dessert dish and freeze.

Mango
Raspberry Ice

2 c. raspberries
1 mango (peeled & pitted)

Juice the fruits. Pour into dessert dish and freeze.

Strawberry Ice

4 c. strawberries (hulled)

Juice the fruits. Pour into dessert dish and freeze.

Strawberry Pear Sorbet

4 c. strawberries (hulled)
2 pears
1/2 c. agave

Juice the fruits. Place all ingredients in the ice cream maker to freeze.

Mango Sorbet

4 mangos (peeled & pitted)
1/2 c. agave

Juice the fruits. Place both ingredients in the ice cream maker to freeze.

Melon Sorbet

1/4 seedless watermelon (rind removed)
1/2 cantaloupe (peeled & seeded)
1/2 honeydew (rind removed & seeded)
3/4 c. agave

Juice the fruits. Place all ingredients in the ice cream maker to freeze.

Tropical Bliss
Ice Treat

2 c. raspberries
1/4 pineapple (rind removed)
3 blood oranges (peeled)

Juice the fruits separately. Freeze the juice separately in layers.

Island Punch
Ice Treat

2 mangos (peeled & pitted)
2 c. raspberries

Juice the fruits. Freeze then serve.

Lemon Pear
Ice Treat

2 pears
1/2 lemon (peel intact)

Juice the fruits. Freeze then serve.

APPLE SPICE MUFFINS

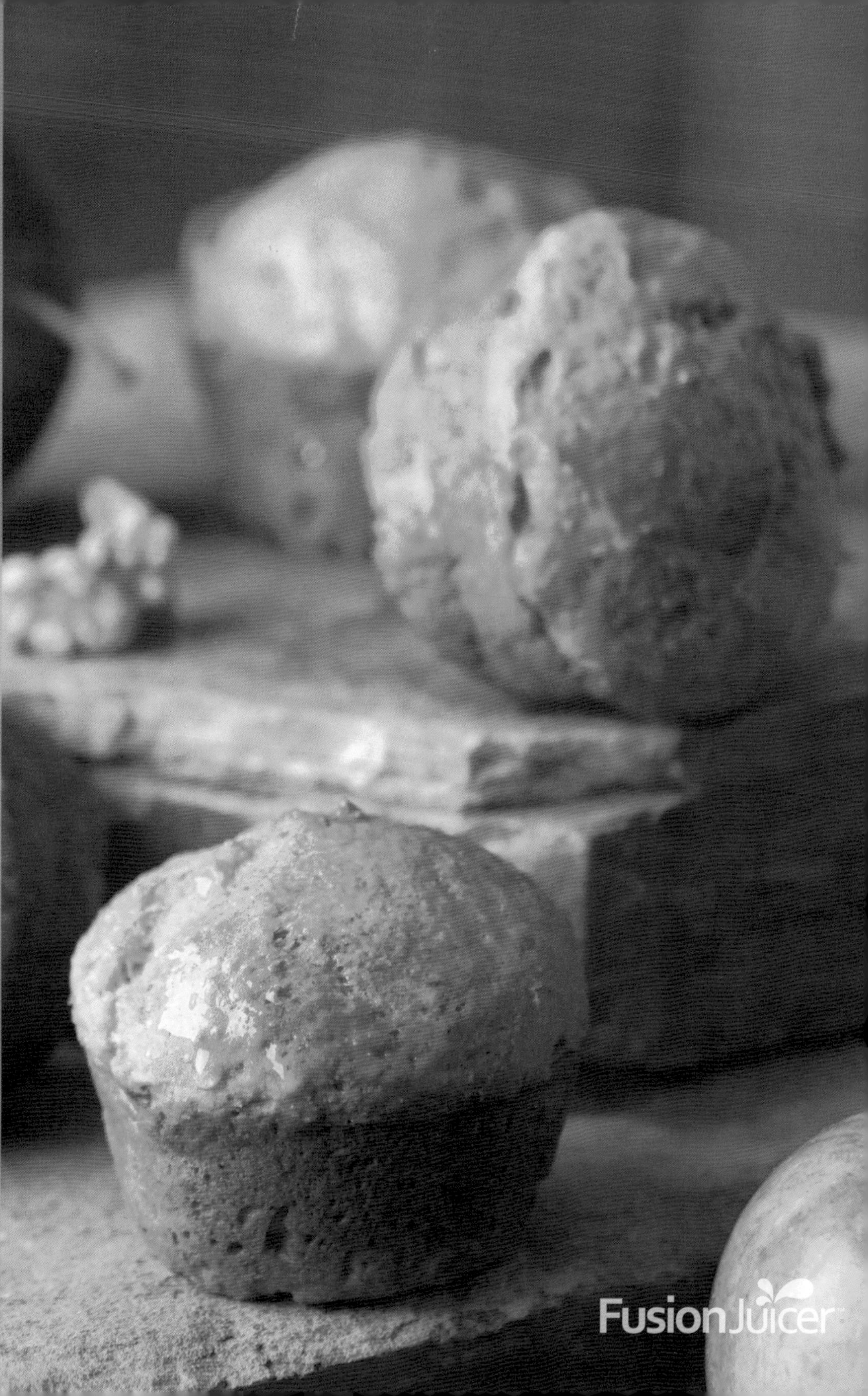

Apple Spice Muffins

1 1/2 c. unbleached flour
1 1/2 c. apple pulp
1/4 c. apple juice
1/2 c. whole-wheat flour
2/3 c. honey
2 tsp. baking powder
1/4 tsp. salt
1/4 tsp. cinnamon
1/2 c. skim milk
2 egg whites

Preheat oven to 400° F. Mixture 1: Combine 1/2 c. of unbleached flour, skim milk, apple pulp and apple juice. Mixture 2: Combine 1 c. unbleached flour, whole-wheat flour, honey, baking powder, salt, cinnamon, and egg whites. Combine mixture 1 and mixture 2, and mix until moistened. Bake at 400° F for approximately 25 minutes.

Orange Macadamia Muffins

2 c. whole-grain flour
3 tbsp. honey
3 tsp. baking powder
1/2 tsp. salt
1 c. orange juice
3 tbsp. canola oil
2 tsp. orange rind pulp
2 egg whites
1/4 c. finely chopped macadamia nuts

Preheat oven to 400° F. Combine flour, baking powder, nuts and salt. Mix well. Combine orange juice, honey, canola oil, orange rind pulp and egg whites. Mix together until dry ingredients are moist. Bake at 400° F for approximately 15–19 minutes.

FusionJuicer™

Autumn Squash Loaf

2 c. whole-grain flour
1/2 tsp. baking soda
2 tsp. cinnamon
1/4 tsp. salt
1 tsp. baking powder
1/2 c. honey
3 tsp. vanilla
2 eggs
1/2 c. canola oil
1 1/2 c. yellow squash pulp
1 1/2 c. mashed or minced dates

Preheat oven 350° F. Grease loaf pan. Beat squash and dates well. Slowly add canola oil and blend well. Slowly add eggs and vanilla continue to beat mixture. Combine all remaining ingredients to mixture. Gently blend. Fill loaf pan. Bake approximately 1 hour.

Zucchini Orange Bread

4 eggs
1 3/4 c. honey
3/4 c. canola oil
2/3 c. orange juice
2 c. zucchini pulp
3 1/4 c. whole-grain flour
1 1/2 tsp. baking powder
1 1/2 tsp. baking soda
1 tsp. salt
2 1/2 tsp. cinnamon
1/2 tsp. cloves
2 tsp. grated orange peel
1/2 c. chopped walnuts

Preheat oven to 350° F. Grease loaf pan. In a large bowl beat eggs. Add honey, orange juice, oil and zucchini until blended. Add all remaining ingredients and mix well. Fill loaf pan. Baking time approximately 45–55 minutes.

BERRY SURPRISE MUFFINS

FusionJuicer

Berry Surprise Muffins

2 c. whole-grain flour
2/3 c. honey
3 tsp. baking powder
1 tsp. lemon or orange pulp
1/2 c. orange juice
1/2 tsp. salt
2 egg whites
3/4 c. blueberries
3/4 c. raspberry pulp
1/4 c. raspberry juice

Preheat oven to 400° F. Mixture 1: Combine whole-grain flour, honey, baking powder, lemon or orange pulp. Mix thoroughly. Mixture 2: Combine orange juice, canola oil, egg whites, raspberry juice and raspberry pulp. Mix thoroughly. Combine mixture 1 and 2 together. Gently stir in fresh blueberries. Grease muffin pan and fill muffin pan. Bake for approximately 20–25 minutes.

Basic Berry Muffins

1 c. oats
3 3/4 tsp. lemon juice
1 1/4 c. 1% or skim milk
1/2 c. honey
1/4 c. canola oil
1 egg slightly beaten
1 1/2 c. whole-wheat flour
1 tsp. baking soda
1/2 c. berry pulp (berry of your choice)
1/4 c. berry juice

Preheat oven to 375° F. Combine oats, lemon juice and milk. Blend well. Set aside for about 5 minutes. Grease muffin pan. Mix honey, egg and oil to milk mixture. Blend well. Combine flour and baking soda. Add to milk mixture just until moist. Stir in berry pulp and berry juice. Fill muffin pan. Bake at 375° F for 20–25 minutes.

EASY CARROT CAKE

Fusion Cutter

Easy Carrot Cake

3 1/2 c. carrot pulp
1/2 c. apple pulp
3 c. whole-grain flour
1 c. canola oil
3 eggs
1 c. honey
1 tbsp. baking soda
2 tbsp. cinnamon
2 tsp. nutmeg
1 tbsp. vanilla
1 1/2 c. crushed walnuts

*Preheat oven to 350° F. Blend oil, carrot and apple pulp together.
Add honey, eggs and vanilla to pulp mixture. Sift all dry ingredients and mix with pulp.
Add nuts and mix. Grease pan. Fill pan and bake. Bake approximately 1 hour.*

Sweet Potato Bread

2 1/3 c. honey
1/3 c. water
1/3 c. sweet-potato juice
2/3 c. canola oil
4 eggs
2 c. sweet-potato pulp
3 1/3 c. whole-grain flour
2 tsp. baking soda
1 1/2 tsp. salt
1 tsp. cinnamon
1/2 tsp. baking powder
1 c. chopped pecans

*Preheat oven to 350° F. Combine honey, water, sweet-potato juice, eggs, oil
and sweet-potato pulp. Mix well. Add flour, baking soda, cinnamon, baking powder and salt.
Mix until dry ingredients are moist. Bake approximately 1 hour.*

HONEY ZUCCHINI BREAD

FusionJuicer

Honey Zucchini Bread

3 eggs
1 c. canola oil
1 c. honey
2 c. zucchini pulp
2 tsp. baking powder
2 tsp. salt
1/2 c. wheat germ
1 1/2 c. oat flour
1 c. chopped walnuts

*Preheat oven to 350° F. Mixture 1: Beat eggs, add oil and honey. Beat until thick.
Then, mix in zucchini pulp. Mixture 2: Add flour, wheat germ,
baking powder and walnuts. Add mixture 1 and mixture 2 together.
Pour into 2 greased loaf pans. Bake for approximately 1 hour.*

Orange Carrot Bread

3/4 c. carrot pulp
2/3 c. honey
1/4 c. orange juice
1 tbsp. canola oil
2 egg whites
3/4 c. whole-wheat flour
2 tsp. baking powder

*Preheat oven to 400° F. Combine carrot pulp, honey, orange juice, oil, and egg whites.
Mix well. Next add flour and baking powder. Mix until all ingredients
are incorporated. Bake for approximately 15–20 minutes.*

ORANGE GINGER CRAN COOKIES

Orange Ginger
Cran Cookies

1/2 c. orange, lemon, & ginger pulp
3/4 c. butter substitute
3/4 c. organic brown sugar
1 c. oats
2 c. whole-wheat flour
1 tsp. baking soda
1/3 c. dried cranberries
1 egg

Preheat oven to 375° F degrees. Place the butter substitute, egg and brown sugar in a mixer until creamy. Add all remaining ingredients. Mix well. On 2 large, non-stick cookie sheet pans, use about a 2 tbsp. ice cream scoop to drop cookies onto the cookie sheet pan. Bake about 12–14 minutes, or until golden brown around the edges. Cool completely on wire rack before serving.
Makes about 2 dozen cookies

Orange
Cranberry Muffins

2 c. oat flour
4 tbsp. honey
4 tsp. baking powder
1/2 tsp. salt
1 c. fresh orange juice
3 tbsp. canola oil
2 tsp. orange pulp
2 egg whites
1/2 c. fresh cranberries

Preheat oven 400° F. Grease muffin cups. Combine all dry ingredients. Mix well. In separate bowl combine orange juice, oil, orange pulp and egg whites to dry ingredients. Stir just until ingredients are moistened. Fill muffin pan with mixture. Bake 400° F for 14–18 minutes.

JUICY PEAR MUFFINS

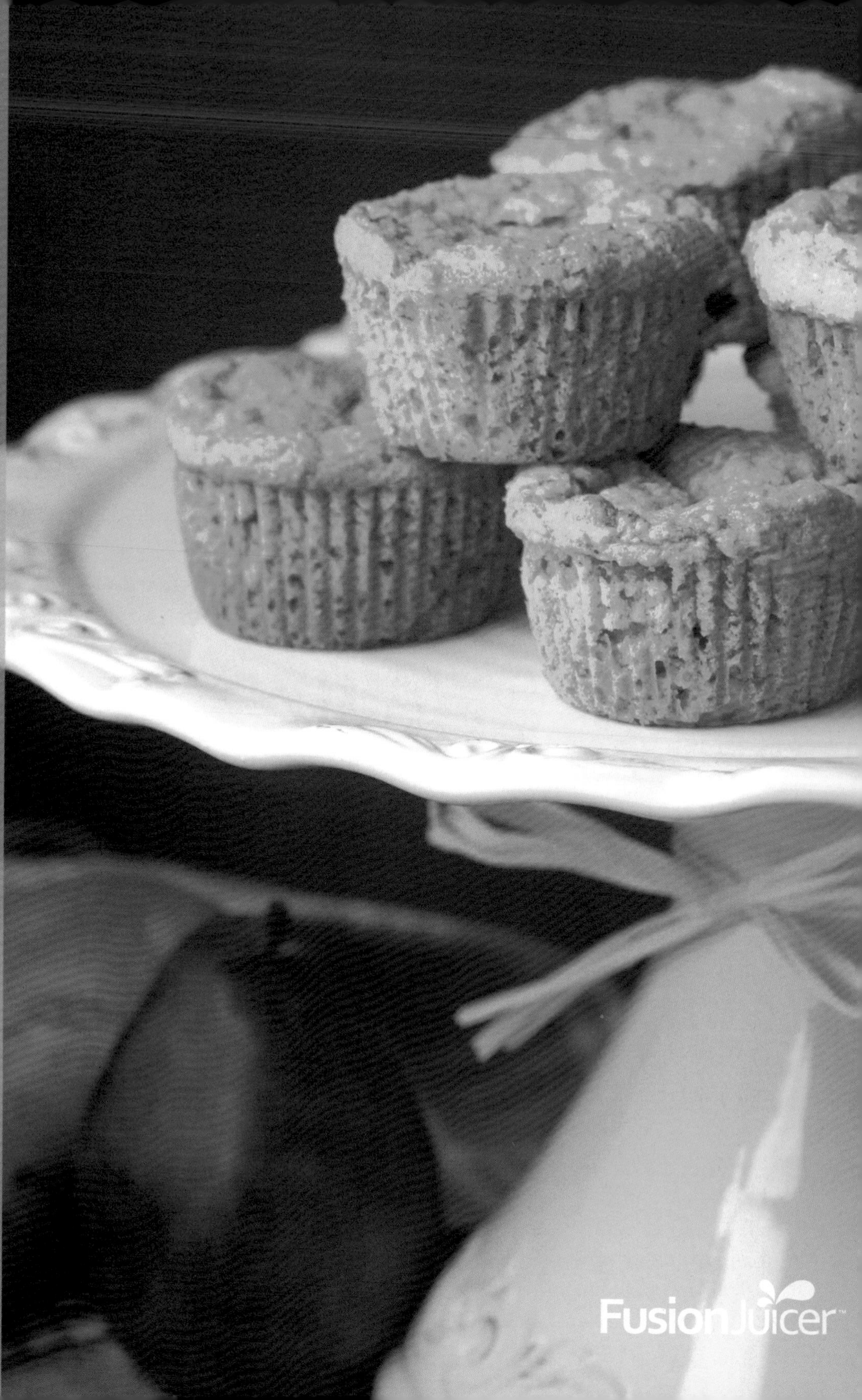

Juicy Pear Muffins

1 3/4 whole-wheat flour
1/2 c. honey
4 tsp. baking powder
1/4 tsp. salt
1 tsp. cardamom
1 1/2 c. pear pulp
1/2 c. pear juice
1/2 c. skim milk
3 tbsp. canola oil
2 egg whites

Preheat oven 400° F. Grease muffin pan. Combine all dry ingredients. Add pear pulp into flour mixture. In separate bowl, mix milk, oil, egg whites, and pear juice. Blend well. Stir into dry ingredients. Do not over mix. Fill muffin pan. Bake at 400° F for 15–20 minutes.

Lemon Raspberry Muffins

1/2 c. vanilla yogurt
3 tbsp. canola oil
1 tbsp. lemon juice
1 egg
1 1/2 c. whole-grain flour
1/2 c. honey
1/4 tsp. salt
2 1/2 tsp. baking powder
1 tsp. lemon pulp
1/2 c. raspberry pulp
1 tsp. vanilla extract
1/4 c. raspberry juice

Preheat oven to 400° F. Mixture 1: Combine yogurt, oil, lemon juice and egg. Blend thoroughly. Mixture 2: Combine whole-grain flour, honey, baking powder, lemon pulp, raspberry pulp and raspberry juice. Add mixture 1 to mixture 2 stir until moistened. Grease muffin pan. Bake at 400° F for 20 minutes.

STRAWBERRY PAPAYA MACAROON

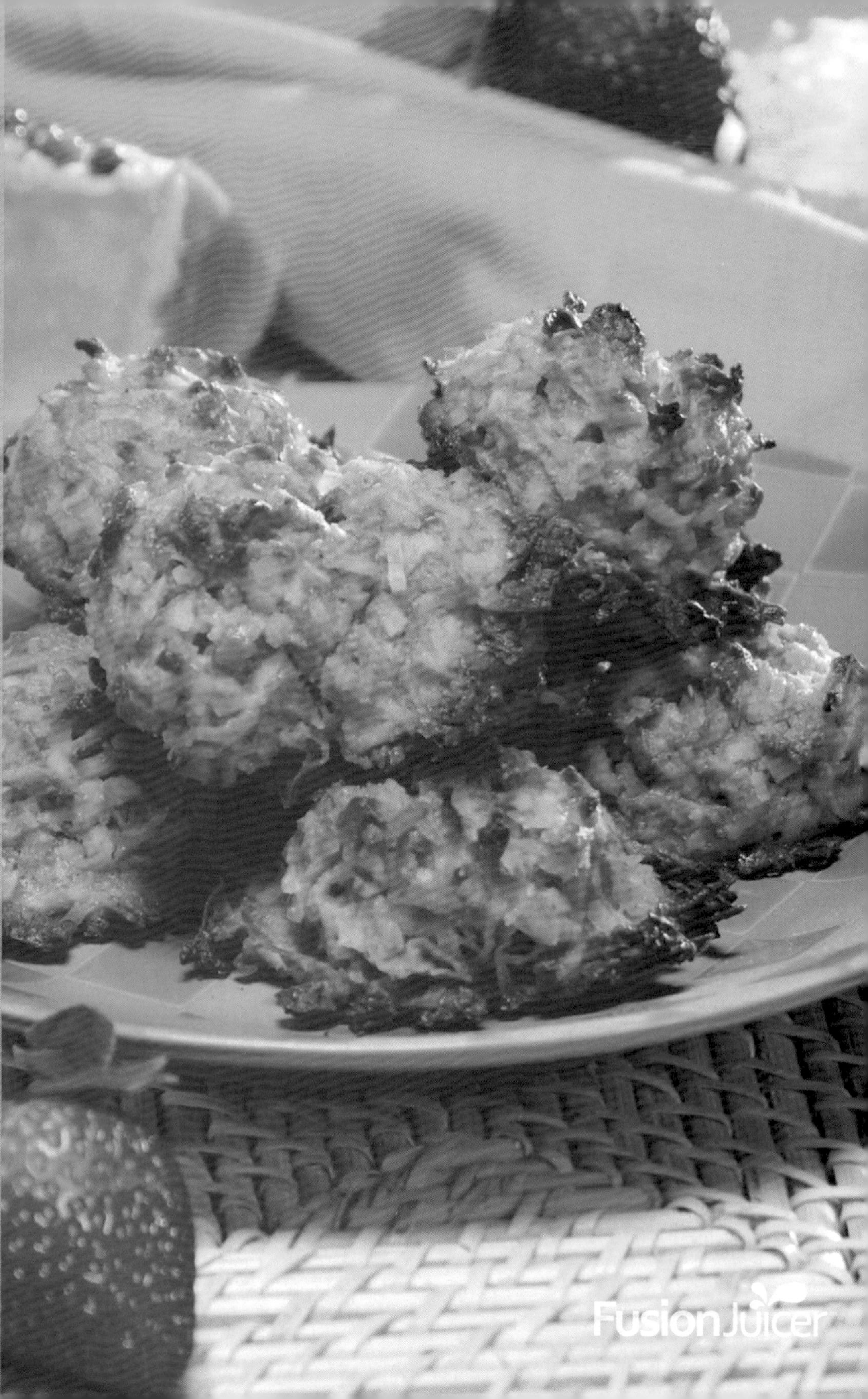

Strawberry Papaya Macaroons

1/2 c. strawberry & papaya pulp from
[1 papaya (peeled & seeded) & 1 pt. strawberries (hulled)]
1/2 c. organic brown sugar
3 c. coconut (shredded)
2 egg whites
1/4 c. whole-wheat flour

*Preheat oven to 375˚ F. In a bowl, mix all ingredients together. Use 2 tbsp.
ice cream scoop to drop macaroons onto a large, non-stick cookie-sheet pan.
Bake about 12 –14 minutes, or until golden brown around the edges. Cool completely
on wire rack before serving.*
Makes about 10-12 cookies

Golden Carrot Muffins

3 c. whole-grain flour
1 tbsp. baking soda
3 1/2 c. carrot pulp
1 c. pineapple pulp
1 c. honey
2 tbsp. cinnamon
1 tsp. nutmeg
6 egg whites
1 tbsp. vanilla
1 c. canola oil
1 1/2 c. crushed walnuts

*Preheat oven to 350˚ F. Grease muffin pan. Mix together dry ingredients. Combine egg whites,
vanilla, honey, and oil. Add to dry ingredients. Add carrot and pineapple pulp to mixture,
then add nuts. Fill muffin pan. Bake 45 minutes.*

STRAWBERRY MANGOLICIOUS MUFFINS

FusionJuicer™

Strawberry Mangolicious Muffins

2 c. whole-grain flour
2/3 c. honey
4 tsp. baking powder
3/4 c. 1% or skim milk
1/3 c. canola oil
2 egg whites
1/2 c. strawberry pulp
1/2 c. mango pulp
1/4 c. strawberry juice
1/4 c. mango juice
1/2 tsp. salt

Preheat oven to 375° F. Grease muffin pan. Mix dry ingredients; mix well. Combine honey, milk, oil, and egg whites. Stir well. Add flour mixture until moistened. Gently add pulp and juice. Add mixture to muffin pan. Bake at 375° F for 12–16 minutes. Edges will get light brown. Muffins should cool 3–4 minutes before removing from pan.

Harvest Blend Muffins

2 c. whole-wheat flour
1 1/4 c. honey
2 tsp. baking soda
2 tsp. cinnamon
1/2 tsp. salt
2 c. apple pulp
1/2 c. coconut
1/2 c. raisins
1/2 c. walnuts
3/4 c. canola oil
1/4 c. milk
2 tsp. vanilla
2 eggs

Preheat oven to 350° F. Combine whole-wheat flour, baking soda, cinnamon and salt. Mix well. Stir in apple pulp, coconut, raisins and walnuts. Add oil, milk, vanilla, eggs, and honey. Stir until dry ingredients are moistened. Bake approximately 20–25 minutes.

Balsamic Dressing

1 shallot (peeled)
1/4 onion (peeled)
2 garlic cloves (peeled)
1/2 cup balsamic vinegar
1 tbsp. agave
1 1/4 cup olive oil
sea salt & freshly ground black pepper to taste

*Juice the shallot, onion and the garlic. In a bowl,
add the juice, balsamic vinegar and agave. Slowly add
the olive oil, while mixing to incorporate. Serve over a bed of greens.*

Cilantro Lime Vinaigrette

2 limes (peel intact)
1 bunch cilantro leaves
1/2 c. honey
3 c. olive oil
3 garlic cloves (peeled)
sea salt & freshly ground black pepper to taste

*Juice lime, cilantro, and garlic. In a bowl, combine juice with remaining
ingredients. Mix well. Serve over a bed of greens.*

FusionJuicer™

Orange Vinaigrette

1/2 c. orange juice
1/4 c. orange pulp
1/4 c. white wine vinegar
3/4 c. grapeseed oil
sea salt & freshly ground black pepper to taste

Mix all ingredients well. Serve over your favorite greens.

Pineapple
Mango Vinaigrette

1/4 c. pineapple juice
1/4 c. mango juice
1 tbsp. mango pulp
1 tbsp. pineapple pulp
1/2 c. white wine vinegar
1 c. olive oil
sea salt & freshly ground black pepper to taste

Mix all ingredients well. Serve over your favorite greens.

ORANGE VINAIGRETTE

FusionJuicer™

Raspberry Vinaigrette

1/2 c. raspberry juice
1 tbsp. raspberry pulp
1/4 c. raspberry vinegar
3/4 c. olive oil
sea salt & freshly ground black pepper to taste

Mix all ingredients well. Serve over your favorite greens.

Strawberry Balsamico

1 c. strawberry juice
1 tbsp. strawberry pulp
1/4 c. balsamic vinegar
3/4 c. olive oil
sea salt & freshly ground black pepper to taste

Mix all ingredients well. Serve over your favorite greens.

Fusion Juicer™

Fresh Pasta Salad

1 lb. whole-wheat pasta (cooked & drained)
1/4 c. red bell pepper pulp
1/4 c. yellow bell pepper pulp
1/4 c. asparagus spears
1/4 c. onion pulp
1/2 c. zucchini pulp
1/2 c. carrot pulp
1/2 c. balsamic vinegar
salt and pepper to taste
2 tbsp. olive oil

Mix all ingredients well.

Tomato Stuffed with Broccoli

2 tomatoes
1 c. broccoli pulp
1 tsp. onion pulp
1 tsp. garlic pulp
1 tbsp. white wine vinegar
2 tbsp. extra-virgin olive oil
sea salt & freshly ground black pepper to taste

In a bowl, mix all ingredients except tomatoes.
Stuff the tomatoes with the mixture and serve.

Apple Tarragon Vinaigrette

2 red apples
1 bunch tarragon
2 garlic cloves (peeled)
1/2 c. cider vinegar
2 c. olive oil
sea salt & freshly ground black pepper to taste

*Juice apples, tarragon and garlic. In a bowl, combine juice
with remaining ingredients. Mix well. Serve over a bed of greens.*

CUCUMBER DILL DIP

FusionJuicer™

Cucumber Dill Dip

1 c. plain yogurt
1/2 c. cucumber pulp
1/3 c. cucumber juice
1 tbsp. fresh chopped dill
sea salt & freshly ground pepper to taste

Mix well and serve with crudités.

Dip with a Zip

1 c. tomato pulp
1/2 c. horseradish
2 tbsp. onion pulp
1 c. low-fat yogurt
sea salt & freshly ground pepper to taste

Mix all the ingredients and serve.

FusionJuicer™

Papaya Lime Salsa

1c. papaya pulp
1/4 c. papaya juice
1/8 c. cilantro leaves (chopped)
1/2 lime (peel intact)
1/4 jalapeño pepper (diced)
1/4 red onion (peeled & diced)

Juice papaya and lime separately. In a bowl, mix all the ingredients. Garnish with cilantro and serve.

Mango Salsa

1/4 c. lime juice
1 c. mango pulp
2 tbsp. onion pulp
1/2 tbsp. jalapeño pepper pulp
1 1/2 tsp. honey
1/8 c. cilantro (chopped)
freshly ground pepper & salt to taste

Mix well and serve with fish.

FusionJuicer™

Simply Salsa

2 c. tomato pulp
1/4 c. onion pulp
1/4 c. red bell pepper pulp
1 tsp. cilantro (chopped)
1/2 jalapeño (chopped)
sea salt & freshly ground pepper to taste
3/4 c. tomato juice

Mix well and serve with baked tortilla chips.

Mango Pineapple Passion Fruit Salsa

1/2 c. mango pulp
1/2 c. pineapple pulp
1/4 c. passion fruit juice

Mix well. Serve with pear and apple slices.

SUMMER SALSA

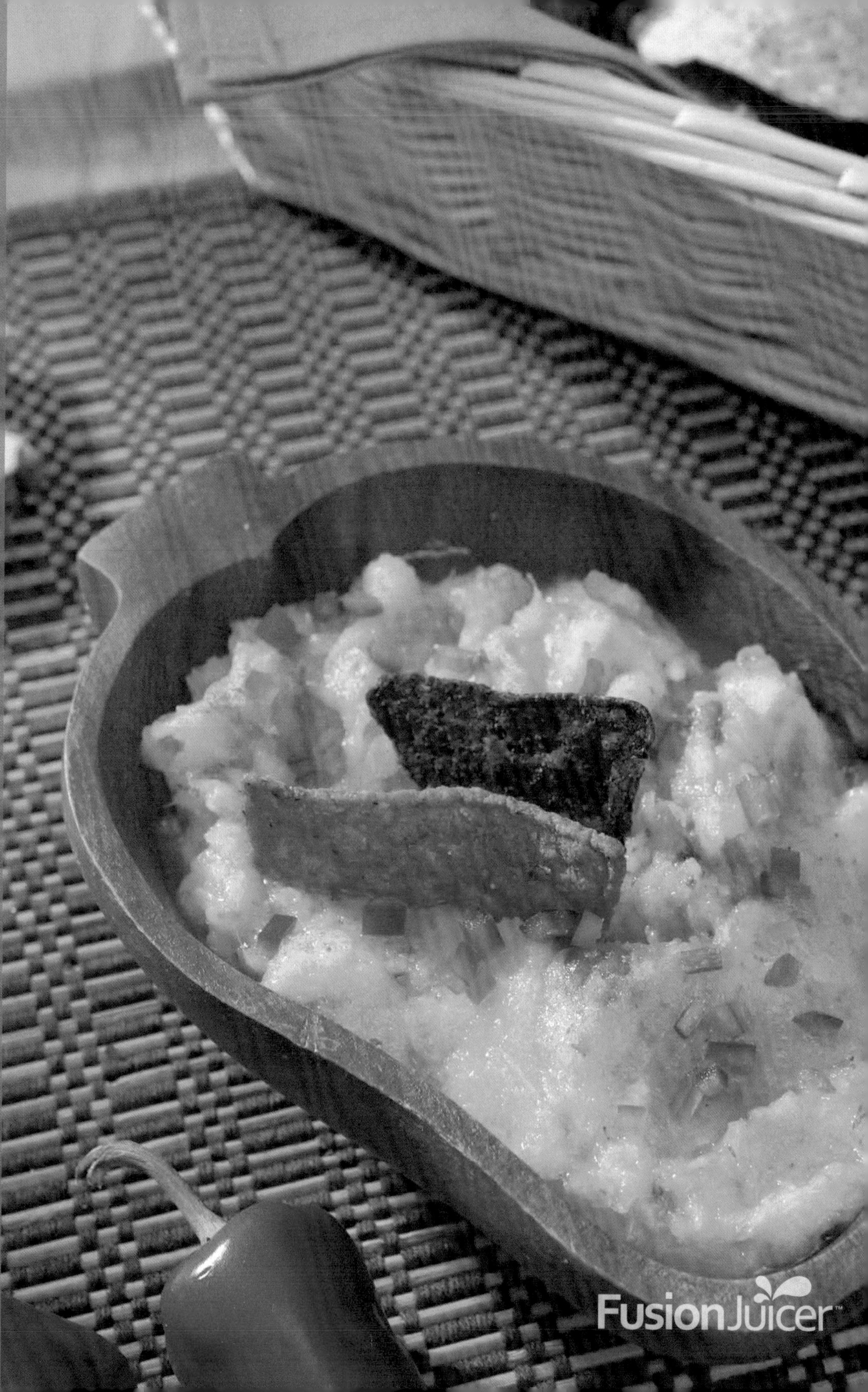

Summer Salsa

1/4 c. orange pulp
1/4 c. pineapple pulp
1/4 jalapeño (chopped)
1/4 red bell pepper pulp
1/4 c. orange & pineapple juice

Mix well. Serve with pear and apple slices.

Raspberry Orange Salsa

1/2 c. orange pulp
1 tbsp. orange juice
1/4 c. raspberry pulp
1 tbsp. raspberry juice

Mix well. Serve with pear and apple slices.

FusionJuicer

Tropical Salsa

1 kiwi (peeled)
1/2 pink grapefruit (peeled)
1/4 pineapple (rind removed)
1/2 jalapeño pepper
1/8 c. cilantro leaves
1/2 lime (peel intact)

*Juice all the ingredients. In a bowl, place pulp collected
from the pulp container and 1/2 cup of juice from juicer.
Mix well and serve.*

Carrot Ginger Soup

2 c. carrot juice
1/2 c. plain yogurt
1 1/2 tbsp. ginger juice
freshly ground black pepper to taste

Mix all ingredients. Chill before serving.

Summer Soup

1/2 c. fresh cantaloupe juice
1/2 c. fresh honeydew juice
1/2 c. plain yogurt
freshly ground black pepper to taste

Mix all ingredients. Chill before serving.

Gazpacho

2 cucumbers (peeled)
8 vine-ripe tomatoes
1 red bell pepper (stemmed & seeded)
2 garlic cloves (peeled)
1 tbsp. cilantro (chopped)
freshly ground black pepper to taste

Juice the first four ingredients. Mix all the ingredients with all the pulp from the juicer. Chill before serving.

CARROT GINGER SOUP

FusionJuicer

Creamy Tomato Basil

2 c. tomato juice
1 tbsp. basil juice
3/4 c. plain yogurt

Mix all ingredients well. Serve chilled or hot. Garnish with fresh basil.

Garden
Vegetable Soup

3 celery stalks
2 medium zucchinis
1 small onion (peeled)
5 medium carrots (tops removed)
sea salt & freshly ground black pepper to taste

*Juice all ingredients except salt and pepper. Add all juice and pulp into pot.
Simmer on low heat for 5 minutes. Serve hot.*

Carrot Apple Soup

2/3 c. carrot juice
1 tsp. carrot pulp
1/2 c. apple juice
1 tsp. apple pulp
1/4 c. walnuts (finely chopped)

Mix well and serve chilled.

CREAMY TOMATO BASIL

Fusion Juicer

Chilled Cucumber Soup

2 cucumbers (peeled)
1/2 red onion (peeled)
2 garlic cloves (peeled)
1 tbsp. red wine vinegar
3/4 c. low-fat yogurt
sea salt & freshly ground black pepper to taste

*Juice first three ingredients. In a bowl, mix the juice and
1/2 the pulp with the remaining ingredients. Chill before serving.*

Cantaloupe Soup

1 cantaloupe (peeled & seeded)
1/2 lime (peel intact)
1/2 c. yogurt

*Juice the cantaloupe and lime. Combine juice
with 1/2 the pulp and yogurt. Mix well and chill before serving.*

Juices (10–137)

Juices (10–137)

RECIPE INDEX

Salsas & Dips (176–185)

Soups (186–190)